How to Start a Construction Business

A Step by Step Guide to Starting a New Construction Company

By Meir Liraz

Published by BizMove
www.bizmove.com

Table of Contents

a. Excel Financial Projections Creator software.
b. Extensive business plan template in MS Word
format.
c. Simple business plan template in MS Word
format
d. Small Business Management: Essential
Ingredients for Success (eBook)
e. Business Plan Training Course (Online Video)

f. How To Find And Attract Investors Training Course (Online Video)

g. How to Start a Small Business Manual (PDF eBook)

h. How to Be a Great Manager and Leader (Video Guide)

i. How to Better Manage Yourself for Success (Video Guide)

1. Things to Consider Before You Start

This guide will walk you step by step through all the essential phases of starting a successful construction business. To profit in a construction based business, you need to consider the following questions: What business am I in? What do I sell? Where is my market? Who will buy? Who is my competition? What is my sales strategy? How much money is needed to operate my firm? How will I get the work done? What management controls are needed? How can they be carried out? When should I revise my plan? Where can I go for help?

No one can answer such questions for you. As the owner-manager you have to answer them and draw up your business plan. The pages of this guide are a combination of text and workspaces so you can write in the information you gather in developing your business plan - a logical progression from a commonsense starting point to a commonsense ending point.

It takes time and energy and patience to draw up a satisfactory business plan. Use this guide to get your ideas and the supporting facts down on paper. And, above all, make changes in your plan on these pages as that plan unfolds and you see the need for changes.

Bear in mind that anything you leave out of the picture will create an additional cost, or drain on your money, when it unexpectedly crops up later on. If you leave out or ignore too many items, your business is headed for disaster.

Keep in mind, too, that your final goal is to put your plan into action. More will be said about this step near the end of this guide.

What's In This For Me?

The hammer, trowel, pliers, and wrench are well known tools of the construction industry. They have their various uses and are needed to get the work done. Management is another tool that the owner-manager of a construction firm must use. Each job must be planned and organized if the firm is to run smoothly and efficiently. The business plan will help you increase your skill as a manager.

Because of the diversification in the construction industry, you may be engaged in residential, commercial, or industrial construction. You may be either a general or specialty contractor. But, the same basic managerial skills are needed. This plan will serve as a guide to the various areas that you as a manager will be concerned with. As you work through this plan, adapt it to your own particular needs.

When complete, your business plan will help guide your daily business activities. When you know where you want to go, it is easier to plan what you must do to get there. Also, the business plan can serve as a communications device which will orient key employees, suppliers, bankers, and whoever else needs to know about your goals and your operations.

Whether you are just thinking about starting your own firm or have already started, the business plan can help you. As your skill as a manager increases so will the number of jobs you can effectively control. The careful completion of this plan may point out your limitations. This is important. To be a successful contractor you must not only know your business thoroughly, but must also know your limitations and seek professional advice in these areas.

Why Am I In Business?

Most contractors are in business to make money and be their own boss. Very important reasons. But, don't forget, no one is likely to stay in business unless you also satisfy a consumer need at a competitive price. Profit is the reward for satisfying consumer needs in a competitive economy.

In the first years of business, your profits may seem like a small return for the long hours, hard work, and responsibility of being the boss. But there are other rewards associated with having your own business. For example, you may find satisfaction in helping to put groceries on your employees' tables. Or, maybe your satisfaction will come from building a business you can pass on to your children.

Why are you in business?

_____

_____

_____

What Business Am I In?

At first glance this may seem like a rather silly question. You may say, "If there is one thing I'm sure of, it's what huskiness I'm in." But wait. Let's look further into the question. Suppose you say, "I build houses." Are you a speculative or custom builder? Are you a remodeler? Are you a subcontractor? Can you schedule a complete job and make money? By planning according to this decision, you should realize the value of this type of thinking in dollars.

Consider this example. Bob Rogers started a small construction business shortly after World War II. Because of Mr. Rogers' skill and talent for design, he directed all his activity toward building taverns. There was enough call for this type of building to keep him and his crew busy until the early 60's. Then sales began to fall off.

By moving his shop to smaller quarter with less overhead and by laying off half his crew, he was able to maintain his business to his satisfaction the rest of his life. After his death, his son examined the situation and decided that he wasn't really in the business of building commercial bars. He was in the business of custom finishing.

Today his business is prospering. He is building cabinets and small bars for private homes. His company also does other finishing work which requires the craftsmanship his crew is capable of.

In the space below, state what business you're really in.

_____

_____

What are your reasons for this opinion?

_____

_____

2. How to Plan Your Marketing

When you have decided what sort of construction business you're really in, you have made your first marketing decision. Now, in order to sell your service or product, you must face other marketing decisions.

Your marketing objective is to find enough jobs at the right times to provide a profitable continuity for your business. Your job starts must be coordinated to eliminate the down time between jobs. In other words, you want to get enough jobs, starting at the right times, to keep from being broke between jobs.

Unless an individual can come up with enough ideas to keep a crew working 12 months a year, maybe he or she is not ready for a construction business.

Where Is Your Market?

Describe your market area in terms of customer profile (age, school needs, income, and so on) and geography. For example, if you are a custom builder, you may decide to build homes in the $180,000 to $500,000 price range. This would mean that your customers will have to have incomes in that class ranges. You may also decide that you can profitable build these homes on the owner's lot if it is located within a radius of 30 miles from your office. (The significance of a customer profile is that it will help you narrow your advertising to those media that will reach the potential customer you have profiled.) In the space below describe your market in terms of customer profile and geography.

My Product / Types of Customers / Location of Customers

_____ _____

_____

_____ _____

_____

Now that you have described what you want in terms of customer and location, what is it about your operation that will make these people want to buy your service?

For instance, quality work, competitive prices, guaranteed completion dates, effective advertising, unique design, and so on.

Write your answer here.

_____

_____

Advertising

You have determined what it is you're marketing, who is going to buy it, and why they're going to buy it. Now you have to decide on the best way to tell your prospective customers about your product.

What should your advertising tell prospective customers?

_____

_____

What form should your advertising take? Ask the local media (newspapers, radio and television stations, and printers of direct mail pieces) for information about their services and the results they offer for your money.

How you spend advertising money is your decision, but don't fall into the trap that snares many advertisers. As one consultant describes this pitfall: It is amazing the way many business managers consider themselves experts on advertising copy and media selection without any experience in these areas.

The following workblock should be useful in determining what advertising is needed to sell your construction service.

Form of Advertising	Size of Audience	Frequency of Use	Cost of a single ad	Est. Cost
_____	_____	_____	_____	____
_____	_____	_____	_____	____
_____	_____	_____	_____	____
_____	_____	_____	_____	____
			Total	____

Competition

The competition in the construction industry often results in low profit margins. However, if you are just starting or are a relatively small firm, this does not put you at a disadvantage. The smaller firm can often compete with the bigger outfit because of lower overhead expense. For example, your office may be in your home, saving that expense. You can often work right out of your truck, saving the expense of a field office.

Competition is largely price competition, although a good reputation for quality and efficiency is beneficial. But, the result of any competition is a high failure rate for poor planners and poor performers. This points out the need for careful planning, particularly in the areas of estimating and bidding.

In order to see what you are up against competitionwise, answer the following questions so you can plan accordingly.

Who will be your major competitors?

_____

_____

How will you compete against them?

_____

_____

Sales Strategy

The market for the construction industry is unique in many ways. As a contractor you will find your market to be dependent on such variables as the state of the economy, local employment stability, the seasonality of the work, labor relations, good subcontractors and interest rates. Also, as a contractor, you will find that you are unavoidably dependent on others, such as customers or financing institutions for payment, and other contractors for performance of their work. You will also want to take your cash flow into consideration when you estimate and bid on a job. The money must come in time to meet your own obligations.

Estimating

whether an owner-manager in the construction business succeeds - makes a profit or not -depends to a great extent on bidding practices. Therefore, you must make careful and complete estimates.

many of the more successful contractors attribute their success to their estimating procedures. They build the job on paper before they submit a bid. In doing this, they break the job down into work units and pieces of material. Then, they assign a cost to each item. The total of these costs will be the direct construction cost. you must also figure on the indirect costs of a job. For instance, you will have overhead expenses such as the cost of maintaining your office, trucks, license fees, and so on. The estimate should also consider any interest charges you will pay on money you borrow to get the job under way. You have insurance fees to pay, surety bond premiums, travel expenses, advertising costs, office salaries, lawyer's fees, and so on. These must also be paid out of your gross income.

Trade associations, as one of their services, often provide their members with a package of business forms. The cost estimate form would be included in this package. The obvious advantage in using these forms is that they are specifically designed for the particular trade.

Regardless of what estimate form you use, it should include such headings as "activity," "material," "labor," "subcontracts," and "estimated cost." And it should have areas for direct construction costs, indirect construction costs, overhead, and profit.

In Addition, a column for the actual cost compared to the estimated cost of a specific work item will make this firm an invaluable record. Here you would have a handy reference to evaluate the profitability of a job after it is complete. It would show you where your estimate was high or low, and enable you to adjust future bids on similar projects. This added column will also be necessary when it comes time for your financial accounting.

Bidding

Your decision to bid or not to bid on a particular job should be determined by several factors. First, do you have the capacity to complete the job on schedule and according to specifications. Beware of overextending yourself out of business. You have to operate within your known capabilities. On any job, you must follow all the details of the work yourself, or find competent supervision.

Planning the Work

When your marketing efforts result in jobs to be done, the problem becomes one of production. How will you plan the work so that the job gets done on time?

No matter how you plan the work, your plan should assist you in two specific ways: (1) it should help you maintain your production schedule, and (2) it should allow you to adjust production to meet changed conditions. such as bad weather.

In planning the work, keep in mind two things: (1) the timing of starts, and (2) the timing of the various steps in the construction of your company. If you have sufficient help and sufficient supervisory personnel, it will be possible for you to engage in as many projects as you can control. The size and nature of the job must be considered here also.

The timing of the steps of constructions (the work scheduling) will show the various operations in sequence and assign a working day designation to each with a space for the calendar day designation. Several operations may be in progress simultaneously. Such a work schedule will show at a glance whether the work is progressing at the right time. Many companies offer commercial scheduling boards designed for this purpose.

Below is a partial work schedule to demonstrate how yours may be set up. Note that there is a column that can be filled in with either a solid mark or an "X" to indicate either partial or completed work. When you look at a particular calendar day, an "X" next to it would indicate that you're on schedule. An open line indicates a delay. Here, then, is a convenient way to see trouble spots that are causing delays and it gives you an opportunity to take corrective action.

Working Day

Activity	Start	Finish	Calendar Day	Complete
1. Layout	1	1	15	x
2. Foundation Forms	1	2	16	x
3. Foundation Pour	3	3	19	___

Working Day

You should save your work schedules. They will form the basis for future estimates. For example, if you are estimating a particular job, you have information on the steps of production, an indication of what materials you'll need and when you'll need them, an indication of how long the job will take, and any peculiarities that may affect the completion of the job. When you consider all these things, you'll be more likely to submit an accurate bid.

By carefully keeping such records, you will also have an indication of how many workers you will need. Perhaps, if the work falls behind schedule, you may need to bring more workers to the job to assure scheduled completion and avoid a possibly larger financial loss from penalization, if that is called for in your contract. Also, such records will give you an indication of the organizational structure you may need for your firm.

Getting the Work Done

If your firm is going to run efficiently, you will need organization. Organization is essential because as your company grows you will not be able to do all the work. You have to delegate work, responsibility, and authority. The organization chart is a useful device in getting this done. It shows quite clearly who is responsible for the major activities of your business.

At first, many construction companies are one man shows. It is up to the owner to do almost everything.

As the company grows, perhaps specialists are added, such as an engineer/estimator, an office manager, and a general superintendent.

What are Your Personnel Requirements?

Will you carry a permanent crew or hire workers as the need arises? _____

How many workers will you need?

_____

What is the hourly rate you will pay?

_____

What will fringe benefits cost?

_____

Will you supervise the work yourself or hire a foreman? If you hire a foreman, what will his salary be?

_____

Will you need clerical help? _____ What will it cost? _____

Equipment

What special equipment will you need (assuming that your work force will supply their own hand tools)?

Equipment	Rent	Buy	Your Cost
_____	_____	_____	_____
_____	_____	_____	_____
_____	_____	_____	_____
_____	_____	_____	_____

Will you need an office or use your home?

_____

_____

If you will need an office, what will the rent and other expenses cost? _____

3. How Much Money Will You Need

Just as with the other aspects of managing a construction business, the basic unit of financial management is the job. The financial aspects of a job must be planned as carefully as the actual construction. The payment for each job must cover the direct and indirect construction costs as well as the allocated share of overhead.

Accounting requirements will vary from company to company and from trade to trade. Your accountant will help you set up the accounting system which will best meet your needs.

However, you must make the overall plans yourself. You must develop the goals necessary to guide and manage your business. This overview will prove invaluable in establishing a good working relationship with your banker (or other lender).

In your financial planning, the first consideration is where the dollars will come from. In dollars, how much business (sales) will you be able to do in the next 12 months? _____

Expenses

In connection with annual sales volume, you need

to think about expenses. For example, if you plan to do $300,000 worth of work, how much will it cost you to do this amount of business? And even more important, what will be left over as profit at the end of the year?

Profit is your pay. Even if you pay yourself a salary for living expenses, your business must make a profit if it is to continue year after year and pay back the money and time you invest in it. Profit helps your firm to be strong - to have a financial reserve for any lean periods.

The "Expenses Worksheet" is designed to help you figure your yearly expenses. To use this worksheet, you need to get one set of figures - the operating ratios for your line of business. If you don't have these figures, check with the trade association which serves your area of the construction industry. Sample Business Plan Construction Company. Construction Business Plan How To.

Expenses Worksheet

Expenses Worksheet

	% of Your sales	Annual sales	Jan	Feb	Mar (etc.)
Sales	100.00%				
Cost of Sales	49.45				
Gross Profit	55.55				
Controllable expenses					
Outside labor	1.15				
Operating supplies	2.34				
Gross wages	22.78				
Repairs and maintenance	0.59				
Advertising	1.12				
Car and delivery	2.04				
Bad debts	0.03				
Administrative and legal	0.48				
Miscellaneous expenses	1.03				
Total controllable expenses	31.56				
Fixed expenses	1				
Rent	1.41				
Utilities	1.16				
Insurance	0.85				
Taxes and licenses	0.10				
Depreciation	1.65				
Total fixed expenses	6.18				
Total expenses	37.74				
net profit (before income tax)	17.81				

Matching Money and Expenses

After you have planned for your month to month expenses, the next question is: Will there be enough money coming in to meet these expenses and to sustain your company in the event that there is down time until your next job?

The cash forecast is a management tool which can eliminate much of the anxiety that can plague you during lean month. Use the worksheet "Estimated Cash Forecast," or ask your accountant to use it, to estimate the amounts of cash that you expect to flow through your business during the next 12 months.

Remember that the expenses of buying the materials and supplies for a particular job may occur a month or two before a payment is made. The "Estimated Cash Forecast" should show this.

Estimated Cash Forecast	Jan Feb Mar Apr May Jun Jul Aug Sep Oct Nov Dec
Expected Available Cash	
Cash Balance	
Expected Receipts	
Job A	
Job B	
Job c	
Bank Loans	
Total Expected Cash	
Expected Cash Requirements	
job A	
Job B	
Job c	
Equipment Payments	
Taxes	
Insurance	
Overhead	
Loan Repayments	
Total Cash Required	
Cash Balance	
Total Loans Due to Bank	

Is Additional Money Needed?

In your planning you may find periods when you will be short of cash. For example, when you start a job you will need materials and supplies. Perhaps it may be a month or two before your first payment. What do you do in the interim if trade credit will not completely satisfy your cash needs?

Your bank may be able to help with a short term loan. If a banker is to lend you money on either a short or long term, he or she will want to know whether your company's financial condition is weak or strong. The bank officer will ask to see a balance sheet.

A blank balance sheet is included. Even if you don't need to borrow, use it. Or, have your accountant use it to draw the "picture" of your firm's financial condition. Moreover, if you don't need to borrow money, you may want to show your plan to the bank that handles your company's account. It is never too early to build good relations with your banker. For the time may come when you will have to borrow.

Control and Feedback

To make your plan work you will need feedback at the various stages of your management process. When you approach a job as a manager, you will need to plan the job, direct the job, and control the job. Throughout this process, you will need adequate financing. Thus, the management controls you set up should supply you with the information you need to keep your operation "on the money."

During the planning stage, you will need to carefully calculate your bid estimate. To direct the job, you will need your job cost analysis to make sure that the job is going to make a profit. And, to control the job, your forces must be organized. This requires the organized production of any given job (work schedule), competent personnel, and your personal follow-up to insure efficient performance.

Is Your Plan Workable?

Now that you've planned this far, step back and take a look at your plan. Is it realistic? Can you do enough business to make a living.

Now is the time to revise your plan if it isn't workable not after you've invested your time and money. If you feel that some revisions are needed before you start your own business, then make them. Go back to the cash flow and adjust the figures. Better, show your plan to someone who has not had a hand in making out your business plan. Your banker, or any outside advisor may be able to point out your strong points which if emphasized could turn into dollars.

If you have strong doubts about your business or your ability to run it, it might be better to delay going into business until you feel as comfortable with the tools of management as you are with the tools of your trade.

Keeping Your Plan Up To Date

How many people in this world can predict the future? Very few indeed! You can expect things to change. You can expect circumstances to be different from what you expected. This is only natural. The difference between successful and unsuccessful planning is often only the ability to keep alert and watch for changes. Stay on top of changing conditions and adjust your plan accordingly. Construction Business Plan How To.

In order to adjust your plan to account for changes, an owner-manager must:

1. Be alert to the changes that come about in your industry, your market, and in your customers.

2. Check your plan against these changes.

3. Determine what revisions, if any, are needed in your plan.

Whatever methods you use to keep up with changing conditions is up to you. Once a month or so, go over your plan. See whether it needs adjusting. If revisions are needed, make them and put them into action.

Put Your Plan Into Action

When your plan is as near on target as possible, you are ready to put it into action. Keep in mind that action is the difference between a plan and a dream. If a plan is not acted upon, it is of no more value than a pleasant dream that evaporates over the breakfast coffee.

The first action step would be acquiring enough capital to get started. Do you already have the money? Will you borrow it from friends, relatives, or a bank? Where and when will you hire competent employees?

What else needs to be done? Look for positive action steps that will get your business rolling. For example, where and how will you get whatever licenses you need to be a contractor?

In the following space, list the things that you must do to get your business off the drawing board and into action. Give each item a date so that it can be done at the right time.

Action / Completion Date

_____/ _____

_____/ _____

_____/ _____

_____/ _____

_____/ _____

4. How to Find New Customers

This guide discusses new customer acquisition. Finding New customers and more sales are essential for profit and growth. The business owner-manager should have a specific program for regularly developing new accounts. This Guide presents a systematic approach to finding, getting, and keeping customers whose sales volume produces profit for you.

Developing New Customer Service

The problem of finding new customers is a common one. A frequent lament of sales managers is "we just don't have enough new accounts to provide the volume we need." In most companies a five percent improvement in sales volume will have a most favorable profit effect. It will equal or exceed, for example, a comparable percentage improvement in costs of material and services, productivity, inventory management or control of receivables.

How to acquire the accounts to provide such added volume becomes a matter of prime importance to survival and growth. In a great many businesses, small and large, the matter of new customer acquisition is approached in a haphazard, intermittent, unplanned and uncoordinated way. The results are understandably often less than satisfying, more expensive than expected, and generally inadequate from the standpoint of contribution of profit.

Useful insight into the problem of getting new customers can be obtained by considering the sales department as a purchasing function, spending company resources by investing in customers and sales volume. The controls, systems, thought, and effort devoted to finding the right source of materials, providing for the most effective delivery performance at a favorable price, is a continuing and evident management concern relative to its purchasing activities. Disciplines are established and controls are in place to measure supplier and purchasing effectiveness. Alternate bids are secured and potential suppliers critically tested for quality and service. Capital expenditures are closely evaluated. Yet the problem of investing to get a new customer, one who is expected to deliver profitable sales over an extended period of time, is often reduced to a simple charge to the sales department of "more new customers!"

In most cases the investment in customer acquisition is heavy, scattered, unmeasured, and unplanned. The moneys spent in this type of effort consist of advertising dollars, sales salaries and expenses, phones, samples, administrative time, and often expensive engineering costs.

The alternative to the shotgun approach to new customer or account development is usually less expensive and substantially more productive. It involves some straightforward initial analysis and planning inexpensive enough for the smallest business. It may likewise involve a change in attitude and emphasis that says that the business of investing in a customer ought to be a selective, investigative, consistent, and planned process, worthy of the closest attention of the managing sales executive. Finding and developing a worthwhile customer is a different objective from simply "more sales" or "more accounts."

The procedure involves ten steps, formalized to the degree necessary for the needs of the enterprise. These are:

1. Specify

2. Quantify

3. Identify

4. Qualify

5. Convince

6. Service

7. Collect

8. Measure

9. Expand

10. Repeat

The first seven are initially critical. A substantial account that does not pay is no "customer."

Specify - Getting New Customers

The first step is to decide what kind of new customer is needed. This involves a brief customer "specification." No one just buys steel or a machine tool or a truck. The kind of steel, its characteristics, its yield are matters of instant concern. Are we trying to buy a simple drill press or a numerically controlled multiple spindle processing unit? Does the truck have to carry one ton or ten tons, and what is to be hauled? Good analysis of the strengths or deficiencies of your present customer accounts can help in preparing your customer specification.

The New Customer Specification Might Read:

Must be within 100 miles. Must be potentially capable of repeat purchases of product "x" totaling $50,000 per year. Must appreciate value of service as opposed to being strictly a price buyer. May be an intermittent process operation where downtime is a critical concern. Frequent changeovers. Quality conscious buyer. Pays promptly on terms. Probably in the Standard Industrial Classification (SIC) or , (describe)

May currently be using product supplied by National or Atlas. Size indicator: at least 100 employees, reasonable in-house maintenance program, evidence of sales growth. Objective: profit contribution rate of 30 percent.

Or the Specification Might Be Simply:

Companies in the meat processing industry, in Michigan, Ohio, Indiana, Kentucky, Pennsylvania (beef, lamb, pork, fowl) engaged in slaughter and/or portion pack, handling over 100 head/day equivalent;

Or:

Independent distributors of products associated with the material handling industry in major trading centers in the southeastern region, having a sales force of no less than five, and carrying recognized domestic truck brands calling on local industry, particularly food processors. Must have repair facilities.

Quantify

How many this quarter or this year? "To provide the type of business required, two new accounts with volume potential of $50,000 each are needed in each of the remaining quarters of the year, plus five new smaller customers in each quarter with a potential of $25,000 to $30,000 annually." Or,

"Need an average of three new small machine accounts each territory, each quarter, with potential of supply sales of $2,500 each per year following installation."

Comment: The new account is admittedly a necessary consideration for growth. Some businesses, however, becomes so concerned with the new account syndrome that they overlook the very real, often untapped, potential of existing accounts. By proper attention to maintenance selling, accounts on the books can be upgraded, expanded to new applications, and in effect become new for all practical purposes. The maintenance aspect of selling is often minimized because the battle has been won - the customer is on the books. Neglect gives your competitors the opportunity to develop a new account by taking away one of your customers. In most cases, developing an existing account is much less costly than acquiring a new customer.

Identify

Having specified and quantified the type and number of new customers wanted, the next step is to identify and rough screen the most likely candidates in the most direct and least expensive way.

A few days devoted to secondary research can prove rewarding. The precise method depends on the scope of the project, the number of required new accounts and the geographic area involved.

For the smaller local business, the telephone directory is an obvious, available, and well organized reference for new accounts. In fact, a study of the directories for several cities provides a fast, comprehensive, and specific source of information for the significant trading centers in a region.

Such listings display products and services offered for sale, the nature of the services offered (like wholesaling, retailing, or manufacturing), the specific location, phone, and zip code reference. If the listings are regarded as definitive of what is sold, they likewise are definitive, with a little deduction, of what such firms buy for resale or as original equipment manufacturers, or for use in their businesses. For example:

Acme Rat Exterminating Products; Rentals, Service, Parts - Rat Poison, Roach Spray, Ant Bait, Bird Repellent, Rat Guards, Animal Traps, Chimney Screens, Sprayers (all types), Electric Fly and Mosquito Killers, etc., including map, address, phone, and brands handled.

Under "Mailing Lists" the yellow pages also give substantial listings of sources who provide listings of various types, often very specific as to Standard Industrial Classification (SIC) number, address, and names of relevant contacts. Purchase of one or more lists across the developed specification provides a fast way to be selective.

All things considered, like today's average cost of $100-$300 for an in-person industrial sales call, the time and money devoted to even modest preplanning data research is well spent.

Lists that can be bought generally key on SIC numbers that, depending on the number of classification digits, give names, size indicators, etc.

Other useful and readily available secondary sources of names are directories of associations, clubs, laboratories, manufacturer, Chamber of Commerce releases, mail order catalogs, and the like. The limit is only imposed by the extent of creative imagination of the researcher. The various desks in the federal and state offices and the public and university libraries are extremely helpful. Often license, permit, and registration data are available and useful.

Basic usage information to identify industries using forgings (by SIC number) was developed from a government report, "Census of Manufacturers."

The scope of companies in those SIC groups was obtained for a specific geographic area from "County Business Patterns." A specific mailing list was then obtained from a directory publisher for specific SIC groups in those area. A rough screening of the list eliminated obvious unlikely prospects (Qualify). Two hundred phone calls were made to the remainder, asking the specific question, "How much do you buy of this type of forging?" Eighty-seven users were identified, large users were coded, and a program of selective selling on twenty-two accounts (some unsuspected users) was undertaken.

Qualify

One of the better sources of new customers among existing users of a product or service is your direct or indirect competitor.

Examination of the sales literature, catalogs, and trade releases of a competitor often reveals a pattern of distribution, a listing of good reference accounts, and often the details of best applications. Review of competitive advertising likewise points up many useful areas of concentration, selling methods, and coverage of what competitors regards to be their major markets.

Placing yourself in the role of a buyer of your own product or service is useful in identifying a competitor's influence points, likely user references, other applications that might not have occurred to you. Your own representatives can be helpful. In other words, shop around for your own product and see who else touches and end users in the distribution process. Each is a potential source of useful information. A frank discussion with some of your good customers will produce names of their competitors who might become your customers as well. Even on a limited local basis such efforts are most rewarding.

Your purchasing agent can be a most useful source of qualifying information because the agent talks to sales-reps who talk to your competitors. In the field of selling, detailed attention to your competitors' activities can be as equally rewarding as attention to your own customers from the standpoint of identifying new customer opportunities, advantages, deficiencies, and needs. The cost is reasonable - an open eye or ear.

When the list is reasonable - identified, broadly qualified and manageable the personal contact or specific qualification phase begins. This takes time, but the effort will be spent on a modest group of targets that have been screened against your broad specification, qualified roughly at minimum cost and have a high probability of productivity.

Good mailing lists tied to selected group targets can help identify new accounts. By a proper offering (i.e., to conduct a free survey, to provide a sample, to solve a specific problem, to offer a study result, to provide a modest prize for best new application, etc.,) a user response can be obtained. From these responses you can qualify the potential of prospective new accounts.

Learning more about your end users can also uncover buyer habits and identifying characteristics indicative of a larger group. For instance, return warranty or registration cards could give you this information from comments or answers to a few basic questions about the product by users. This information can be matched to a larger group, expanding your viewpoint.

Look also for customers among users of alternative products or services to yours. For example, users of plastics are currently converting to die casting for various reasons. Gray iron castings can often be converted to stamped parts or forgings. Automobile buyers are acquiring motor bikes and supermarket shoppers are buying less at the store and eating out more at fast food restaurants. Such habits may bring back some lost customers or make you vulnerable to pressures from the indirect competition.

Convincing a potential user to try your product or service is the next step after you have found and qualified your prospects. This step is the pay off for all your efforts and investment to attract qualified customers. Convincing the potential user to try your product or service is often similar to qualifying customers according to your specifications.

You search in a specific market area for customers that are stable companies with solid needs for your products or services. They will do repeat business and pay their bills. And you are able to come to terms and do business with them.

Keeping customers involves giving service, getting paid, measuring account profitability, expanding customer buying, and then repeating all the steps to get and to keep good customer accounts.

Remember, treat old customers the way you service new ones and you may not need so many new ones.

The Profit Evaluation

How did you do against the measure you set for yourself? Is the trend better? Are your new customers delivering the quality of volume that you want? Tracking your progress is very important. Let's say you were shooting for no increase in fixed costs and $70,000 more profit contribution on the bottom line from new accounts.

There is more to getting new customers than just chasing the volume they produce. Obviously the quality of the volume is more important. Measure your required standard, not just for the amount, but for the profit yield of the volume and the trend for the future.

The new customer development method proposed here emphasized the who, what, why, when and where of volume rather than merely the how much. This takes thoughtful planning, detailed research and screening and some expense but you do get profitable results.

5. Checklist for Starting a Business

Starting a new small business is the dream of many people ... starting that business converts your dream into reality. But there is a gap between your dream and reality that can only be filled with careful planning. As a business owner, you will need a plan to avoid pitfalls, to achieve your goals and to build a profitable business. here are some useful starting businesses tips.

The "Checklist for Going into Business" is a guide to help you prepare a comprehensive business plan and determine if your idea is feasible, to identify questions and problems you will face in converting your idea into reality and to prepare for starting your business.

Operating a successful small business will depend on:

a practical plan with a solid foundation;

dedication and willingness to sacrifice to reach your goal;

technical skills; and

basic knowledge of management, finance, record keeping and market analysis.

As a new owner, you will need to master these skills and techniques if your business is to be successful.

Identify Your Reasons

As a first and often overlooked step, ask yourself why you want to own your own business. Check the reasons that apply to you.

1. Freedom from the 9-5 daily work routine. ____

2. Being your own boss. ____

3. Doing what you want when you want to do it. ____

4. Improving your standard of living. ____

5. Boredom with your present job. ____

6. Having a product or service for which you feel there is a demand. ____

Some reasons are better than others, none are wrong; however, be aware that there are trade-offs. For example, you can escape the 9 to 5 daily routine, but you may replace it with a 6 a.m. to 8 p.m. routine.

A Self-Analysis

Going into business requires certain personal characteristics. This portion of the checklist deals with you, the individual. These questions require serious thought. Try to be objective. Remember, it is your future that is at stake!

Personal Characteristics

Answer each question with Yes or No

1. Are you a leader?

2. Do you like to make your own decisions?

3. Do others turn to you for help in making decisions?

4. Do you enjoy competition?

5. Do you have will power and self discipline?

6. Do you plan ahead?

7. Do you like people?

8. Do you get along well with others?

Personal Conditions

This next group of questions though brief is vitally important to the success of your plan. It covers the physical emotional and financial strains you will encounter in starting a new business.

Are you aware that running your own business may require working 12-16 hours a day six days a week and maybe even Sundays and holidays?

Do you have the physical stamina to handle the workload and schedule?

Do you have the emotional strength to withstand the strain?

Are you prepared if needed to temporarily lower your standard of living until your business is firmly established?

Is your family prepared to go along with the strains they too must bear?

Are you prepared to lose your savings?

Personal Skills And Experience

Certain skills and experience are critical to the success of a business. Since it is unlikely that you possess all the skills and experience needed you'll need to hire personnel to supply those you lack. There are some basic and special skills you will need for your particular business.

By answering the following questions you can identify the skills you possess and those you lack (your strengths and weaknesses).

Do you know what basic skills you will need in order to have a successful business?

Do you possess those skills?

When hiring personnel will you be able to determine if the applicants' skills meet the requirements for the positions you are filling?

Have you ever worked in a managerial or supervisory capacity?

Have you ever worked in a business similar to the one you want to start?

Have you had any business training in school?

If you discover you don't have the basic skills needed for your business will you be willing to delay your plans until you've acquired the necessary skills?

Finding a Niche

Small businesses range in size from a manufacturer with many employees and millions of dollars in equipment to the lone window washer with a bucket and a sponge. Obviously the knowledge and skills required for these two extremes are far apart but for success they have one thing in common: each has found a business niche and is filling it.

The most critical problems you will face in your early planning will be to find your niche and determine the feasibility of your idea. "Get into the right business at the right time" is very good advice but following that advice may be difficult. Many entrepreneurs plunge into a business venture so blinded by the dream that they fail to thoroughly evaluate its potential.

Before you invest time effort and money the following exercise will help you separate sound ideas from those bearing a high potential for failure.

Is Your Idea Feasible?

Identify and briefly describe the business you plan to start.

Identify the product or service you plan to sell.

Does your product or service satisfy an unfilled need?

Will your product or service serve an existing market in which demand exceeds supply?

Will your product or service be competitive based on its quality selection price or location?

Answering yes to any of these questions means you are on the right track; a negative answer means the road ahead could be rough.

Market Analysis

For a small business to be successful the owner must know the market. To learn the market you must analyze it a process that takes time and effort. You don't have to be a trained statistician to analyze the marketplace nor does the analysis have to be costly.

Analyzing the market is a way to gather facts about potential customers and to determine the demand for your product or service. The more information you gather the greater your chances of capturing a segment of the market. Know the market before investing your time and money in any business venture.

These questions will help you collect the information necessary to analyze your market and determine if your product or service will sell.

1. Do you know who your customers will be?

2. Do you understand their needs and desires?

3. Do you know where they live?

4. Will you be offering the kind of products or services that they will buy?

5. Will your prices be competitive in quality and value?

6. Will your promotional program be effective?

7. Do you understand how your business compares with your competitors?

8. Will your business be conveniently located for the people you plan to serve?

9. Will there be adequate parking facilities for the people you plan to serve?

This brief exercise will give you a good idea of the kind of market planning you need to do. An answer of no indicates a weakness in your plan so do your research until you can answer each question with a "yes".

Planning Your Start-up

So far this checklist has helped you identify questions and problems you will face converting your idea into reality and determining if your idea is feasible. Through self-analysis you have learned of your personal qualifications and deficiencies and through market analysis you have learned if there is a demand for your product or service.

The following questions are grouped according to function. They are designed to help you prepare for "Opening Day".

Name and Legal Structure

1. Have you chosen a name for your business?

2. Have you chosen to operate as sole proprietorship partnership or corporation?

Your Business and the Law

A person in business is not expected to be a lawyer but each business owner should have a basic knowledge of laws affecting the business. Here are some of the legal matters you should be acquainted with:

1. Do you know which licenses and permits you may need to operate your business?

2. Do you know the business laws you will have to obey?

3. Do you have a lawyer who can advise you and help you with legal papers?

4. Are you aware of

Occupational Safety and Health requirements?

Regulations covering hazardous material?

Local ordinances covering signs snow removal etc.?

Tax Code provisions pertaining to small business?

Workmen's Compensation laws?

Protecting Your Business

It is becoming increasingly important that attention be given to security and insurance protection for your business. There are several areas that should be covered. Have you examined the following categories of risk protection?

Fire

Theft

Robbery

Vandalism

Accident liability

Discuss the types of coverage you will need and make a careful comparison of the rates and coverage with several insurance agents before making a final decision.

Business Premises and Location

1. Have you found a suitable building in a location convenient for your customers?

2. Can the building be modified for your needs at a reasonable cost?

3. Have you considered renting or leasing with an option to buy?

4. Will you have a lawyer check the zoning regulations and lease?

Merchandise

Have you decided what items you will sell or produce or what service(s) you will provide?

Have you made a merchandise plan based upon estimated sales to determine the amount of inventory you will need to control purchases?

Have you found reliable suppliers who will assist you in the start-up?

Have you compared the prices quality and credit terms of suppliers?

Business Records

Are you prepared to maintain complete records of sales income and expenses accounts payable and receivables?

Have you determined how to handle payroll records tax reports and payments?

Do you know what financial reports should be prepared and how to prepare them?

Finances

A large number of small businesses fail each year. There are a number of reasons for these failures but one of the main reasons is insufficient funds. Too many entrepreneurs try to start and operate a business without sufficient capital (money). To avoid this dilemma you can review your situation by analyzing these three questions:

1. How much money do you have?

2. How much money will you need to start your business?

3. How much money will you need to stay in business?

The chart below will help you answer the second question: How much money will you need to start your business? The chart is for a retail business; items will vary for service construction and manufacturing firms.

The answer to the third question (How much money will you need to stay in business?) must be divided into two parts: immediate costs and future costs.

Business Start-up Cost Estimates

Decorating, remodeling

Fixtures, equipment

Installing fixtures, equipment

Services, supplies

Beginning inventory cost

Legal, professional fees

Licenses, permits

Telephone utility deposits

Insurance

Signs

Advertising for opening

Unanticipated expenses

Total start-up costs _____

From the moment the door to your new business opens a certain amount of income will undoubtedly come in. However this income should not be projected in your operating expenses. You will need enough money available to cover costs for at least the first three months of operation. The chart below will help you project your operating expenses on a monthly basis.

Expenses for one month

Your living costs

Employee wages

Rent

Advertising

Supplies

Utilities

Insurance

Taxes

Maintenance

Delivery/transportation

Miscellaneous

Total expenses _____

Now multiply the total of the chart above by three. This is the amount of cash you will need to cover operating expenses for three months. Deposit this amount in a savings account before opening your business. Use it only for those purposes listed in the above chart because this money will ensure that you will be able to continue in business during the crucial early stages.

By adding the total start-up costs to the total expenses for three months (three times the total cost on The chart above) you can learn what the estimated costs will be to start and operate your business for three months. By subtracting the totals of the charts from the cash available you can determine the amount of additional financing you may need if any. Now you will need to estimate your operating expenses for the first year after start-up.

The first step in determining your annual expenses is to estimate your sales volume month by month. Be sure to consider seasonal trends that may affect your business. Information on seasonal sales patterns and typical operating ratios can be secured from your trade associations.

(NOTE: The relationships among amounts of capital that you invest levels of sales each of the cost categories the number of times that you will sell your inventory (turnover) and many other items form "financial ratios." These ratios provide you with extremely valuable checkpoints before it's too late to make adjustments. In the reference section of your local library are publications such as "The Almanac of Business and Industrial Financial Ratios" to compare your performance with that of other similar businesses.

Next determine the cost of sales. The cost of sales is expressed in dollars. Fill out each month's column in dollars total them in the annual total column and then divide each item into the total net sales to produce the annual percentages. Examples of operating ratios include cost of sales to sales and rent to sales.

After Start-up

The primary source of revenue in your business will be from sales but your sales will vary from month to month because of seasonal patterns and other factors. It is important to determine if your monthly sales will produce enough income to pay each month's bills.

An estimated cash flow projection will show if the monthly cash balance is going to be subject to such factors as:

Failure to recognize seasonal trends;

Excessive cash taken from the business for living expenses;

Too rapid expansion; and

Slow collection of accounts if credit is extended to customers.

Use the following chart to build a worksheet to help you with this problem. In this example all sales are made for cash.

Start New Small Businesses - Conclusion

Beyond a doubt preparing an adequate business plan is the most important step in starting a new business. A comprehensive business plan will be your guide to managing a successful business. The business plan is paramount to your success. It must contain all the pertinent information about your business; it must be well written factual and organized in a logical sequence. Moreover it should not contain any statements that cannot be supported.

If you have carefully answered all the questions on this checklist and completed all the worksheets you have seriously thought about your goal. But . . . there may be some things you may feel you need to know more about.

Owning and running a business is a continuous learning process. Research your idea and do as much as you can yourself but don't hesitate to seek help from people who can tell you what you need to know.

6. How to Get a Business loan

This guide discusses Getting Loans for Business and Small Business Loans to Start Business. Some business persons cannot understand why a lending institution refused to lend them money. Others have no trouble getting funds, but are surprised to find strings attached to their loans. Such owner-managers fail to realize that banks and other lenders have to operate by certain principles just as do other types of business.

This guide discusses the following fundamentals of borrowing: (1) credit worthiness, (2) kinds of loans, (3) amount of money needed, (4) collateral, (5) loan restrictions and limitation, (6) the loan application, and (7) standards which the lender uses to evaluate the application.

Introduction to Getting Loans for Business

Inexperience with borrowing procedures often created resentment and bitterness. The stories of three business persons illustrate this point.

"I'll never trade here again," Bill Smith said when his bank refused to grant him a loan. "I'd like to let you have it, Bill," the banker said, "but your firm isn't earning enough to meet your current obligations." Mr. Smith was unaware of a vital financial fact, namely, that lending institutions have to be certain that the borrower's business can repay the loan

Tom Jones lost his temper when the bank refused him a loan because he did not know what kind of or how much money he needed. "We hesitate to lend," the banker said, "to business owners with such vague ideas of what and how much they need."

John Williams' case was somewhat different. He didn't explode until after he got the loan. When the papers were ready to sign, he realized that the loan agreement put certain limitations on his business activities. "You can't dictate to me," he said and walked out of the bank. What he didn't realize was that the limitations were for his good as well as for the bank's protection.

Knowledge of the financial facts of business life could have saved all three the embarrassment of losing their tempers. Even more important, such information would have helped them to borrow money at a time when their businesses needed it badly.

This guide is designed to give the highlights of what is involved in sound business borrowing. It should be helpful to those who have little or no experience with borrowing. More experienced owner-managers should find it useful in re-evaluating their borrowing operations.

Is Your Firm Credit Worthy?

The ability to obtain money when you need it is as necessary to the operation of your business as is a good location or the right equipment, reliable sources of supplies and materials, or an adequate labor force. Before a bank or any other lending agency will lend you money, the loan officer must feel satisfied with the answers to the five following questions:

What sort of person are you, the prospective borrower? By all odds, the character of the borrower comes first. Next is your ability to manage your business.

What are you going to do with the money? The answer to this question will determine the type of loan, short or long-term. Money to be used for the purchase of seasonal inventory will require quicker repayment than money used to buy fixed assets.

When and how do you plan to pay it back? Your banker's judgment of your business ability and the type of loan will be a deciding factor in the answer to this question.

Is the cushion in the loan large enough? In other words, does the amount requested make suitable allowance for unexpected developments? The banker decides this question on the basis of your financial statement which sets forth the condition of your business and on the collateral pledged.

What is the outlook for business in general and for your business particularly?

Adequate Financial Data Is a "Must"

The banker wants to make loans to businesses which are solvent, profitable, and growing. The two basic financial statements used to determine those conditions are the balance sheet and profit-and-loss statement. The former is the major yardstick for solvency and the latter for profits. A continuous series of these two statements over a period of time is the principal device for measuring financial stability and growth potential.

In interviewing loan applicants and in studying their records the banker is especially interested in the following facts and figures.

General Information:

Are the books and records up-to-date and in good condition? What is the condition of accounts payable? Of notes payable? What are the salaries of the owner-manager and other company officers? Are all taxes being paid currently? what is the order backlog? What is the insurance coverage?

Accounts Receivable:

Are there indications that some of the accounts receivable have already been pledged to another creditor? What is the accounts receivable turnover? Is the accounts receivable total weakened because many customers are far behind in their payments? Has a large enough reserve been set up to cover doubtful accounts? How much do the largest accounts owe and what percentage of your total accounts does this amount represent?

Inventories:

Is merchandise in good shape or will it have to be marked down? How much raw material is on hand? How much work is in process? How much of the inventory is finished goods?

Is there any obsolete inventory? Has an excessive amount of inventory been consigned to customers? Is inventory turnover in line with the turnover for other businesses in the same industry? Or is money being tied up too long in inventory?

Fixed Assets:

What is the type, age, and condition of the equipment? What are the depreciation policies? What are the details of mortgages or conditional sales contracts? What are the future acquisition plans?

What Kind Of Money?

When you set out to borrow money for your firm, it is important to know the kind of money you need from a bank or other lending institution. There are three kinds of money: short term, term money, and equity capital.

Keep in mind that the purpose for which the funds are to be used is an important factor in deciding the kind of money needed. But even so, deciding what kind of money to use is not always easy. It is sometimes complicated by the fact that you may be using some of the various kinds of money at the same time and for identical purposes.

Keep in mind that a very important distinction between the types of money is the source of repayment. Generally short-term loans are repaid from the liquidation of current assets which they have financed. Long-term loans are usually repaid from earnings.

Short-Term Bank Loans

You can use short-term bank loans for purposes such as financing accounts receivable for, say 30 to 60 days. Or you can use them for purposes that take longer to pay off - such as for building a seasonal inventory over a period of 5 to 6 months. Usually, lenders expect short-term loans to be repaid after their purposes have been served: for example, accounts receivable loans, when the outstanding accounts have been paid by the borrower's customers, and inventory loans, when the inventory has been converted into salable merchandise. Small Business Loans to Start Business

Banks grant such money either on your general credit reputation with an unsecured loan or on a secured loan.

The unsecured loan is the most frequently used form of bank credit for short term purposes. You do not have to put up collateral because the bank relies on your credit reputation.

The secured loan involves a pledge of some or all of your assets. The bank requires security as a protection for its depositors against the risks that are involved even in business situations where the chances of success are good.

Term Borrowing

Term borrowing provides money you plan to pay back over a fairly long time. Some people break it down into two forms: (1) intermediate - loans longer than 1 year but less than 5 years, and (2) long-term - loan for more than 5 years.

However, for your purpose of matching the kind of money to the needs of your company, think of term borrowing as a kind of money which you probably will pay back in periodic installments from earnings.

Equity Capital

Some people confuse term borrowing and equity (or investment) capital. Yet there is a big difference. You don't have to repay equity money. It is money you get by selling a part interest in your business.

You take people into your company who are willing to risk their money in it. They are interested in potential income rather than in an immediate return on their investment.

How Much Money?

The amount of money you need to borrow depends on the purpose for which you need funds. Figuring the amount of money required for business construction, conversion, or expansion - term loans or equity capital - is relatively easy. Equipment manufacturers, architects, and builders will readily supply you with cost estimates. On the other hand, the amount of working capital you need depends upon the type of business you're in. While rule-of-thumb ratios may be helpful as a starting point, a detailed projection of sources and uses of funds over some future period of time - usually for 12 months - is a better approach. In this way, the characteristics of the particular situation can be taken into account. Such a projection is developed through the combination of a predicted budget and a cash forecast.

The budget is based on recent operating experience plus your best judgment of performance during the coming period. The cash forecast is your estimates of cash receipts and disbursements during the budget period. Thus, the budget and the cash forecast together represent your plan for meeting your working capital requirements.

To plan your working capital requirements, it is important to know the "cash flow" which your business will generate. This involves simply a consideration of all elements of cash receipts and disbursements at the time they occur. These elements are listed in the profit-and-loss statement which has been adapted to show cash flow. They should be projected for each month.

What Kind of Collateral?

Sometimes, your signature is the only security the bank needs when making a loan. At other times, the bank requires additional assurance that the money will be repaid. The kind and amount of security depends on the bank and on the borrower's situation.

If the loan required cannot be justified by the borrower's financial statements alone, a pledge of security may bridge the gap. The types of security are: endorsers; comakers and guarantors; assignment of leases; trust receipts and floor planning; chattel mortgages; real estate; accounts receivables; saving accounts; life insurance policies; and stocks and bonds. In a substantial number of States where the Uniform Commercial Code has been enacted, paperwork for recording loan transactions will be greatly simplified.

Endorsers, Co-makers, and Guarantors

Borrowers often get other people to sign a note in order to bolster their own credit. These endorsers are contingently liable for the note they sign. If the borrower fails to pay up, the bank expects the endorser to make the note good. Sometimes, the endorser may be asked to pledge assets or securities too.

A co-maker is one who creates an obligation jointly with the borrower. In such cases, bank can collect directly from either the maker or the co-maker.

A guarantor is one who guarantees the payment of a note by signing a guaranty commitment. Both private and government lenders often require guarantees from offices of corporations in order to assure continuity of effective management. Sometimes, a manufacturer will act as guarantor for customers.

Assignment of Leases

The assigned lease as security is similar to the guarantee. It is used, for example, in some franchise situations.

The bank lends the money on a building and takes a mortgage. Then the lease, which the dealer and the parent franchise company work out, is assigned so that the bank automatically receives the rent payments. In this manner, the bank is guaranteed repayment of the loan.

Warehouse Receipts

Banks also take commodities as security by lending money on a warehouse receipt. Such a receipt is usually delivered directly to the bank and shows that the merchandise used as security either has been placed in a public warehouse or has been left on your premises under the control of one of your employees who is bonded (as in field warehousing). Such loans are generally made on staple or standard merchandise which can be readily marketed. The typical warehouse receipt loan is for a percentage of the estimated value of the goods used as security.

Trust Receipts and Floor Planning

Merchandise, such as automobiles, appliances, and boats, has to be displayed to be sold. The only way many small marketers can afford such displays is by borrowing money. Such loans are often secured by a note and a trust receipt.

This trust receipt is the legal paper for floor planning. It is used for serial-numbered merchandise. When you sign one, you (1) acknowledge receipt of the merchandise, (2) agree to keep the merchandise in trust for the bank, and (3) promise to pay the bank as you sell the goods.

Chattel Mortgages

If you buy equipment such as a cash register or a delivery truck, you may want to get a chattel mortgage loan. You give the bank a lien on the equipment you are buying.

The bank also evaluates the present and future market value of the equipment being used to secure the loan. How rapidly will it depreciate? Does the borrower have the necessary fire, theft, property damage, and public liability insurance on the equipment? The banker has to be sure that the borrower protects the equipment.

Real Estate

Real estate is another form of collateral for long-term loans. When taking a real estate mortgage, the bank finds out: (1) the location of the real estate, (2) its physical condition, (3) its foreclosure value, and (4) the amount of insurance carried on the property.

Accounts Receivable

Many banks lend money on accounts receivable. In effect, you are counting on your customers to pay your note.

The bank may take accounts receivable on a notification or a non-notification plan. Under the notification plan, the purchaser of the goods is informed by the bank that his or her account has been assigned to it and he or she is asked to pay the bank. Under the non-notification plan, the borrower's customers continue to pay you the sums due on their accounts and you pay the bank.

Savings Accounts

Sometimes, you might get a loan by assigning to the bank a savings account. In such cases, the bank gets an assignment from you and keeps your passbook. If you assign an account in another bank as collateral, the lending bank asks the other bank to mark its records to show that the account is held as collateral.

Life Insurance

Another kind of collateral is life insurance. Banks will lend up to the cash value of a life insurance policy. You have to assign the policy to the bank.

If the policy is on the life of an executive of a small corporation, corporate resolutions must be made authorizing the assignment. Most insurance companies allow you to sign the policy back to the original beneficiary when the assignment to the bank ends.

Some people like to use life insurance as collateral rather than borrow directly from insurance companies. One reason is that a bank loan is often more convenient to obtain and usually may be obtained at a lower interest rate.

Stocks and Bonds

If you use stocks and bonds as collateral, they must be marketable. As a protection against market declines and possible expenses of liquidation, banks usually lend no more than 75 percent of the market value of high grade stock. On Federal Government or municipal bonds, they may be willing to lend 90 percent or more of their market value.

The bank may ask the borrower for additional security or payment whenever the market value of the stocks or bonds drops below the bank's required margin.

What Are the Lender's Rules for Getting Loans for Your Business?

Lending institutions are not interested in loan repayments. They are interested in borrowers with healthy profit-making businesses. Therefore, whether or not collateral is required for a loan, they set loan limitation and restrictions to protect themselves against unnecessary risks and at the same time against poor management practices by their borrowers. Often some owner-managers consider loan limitations a burden.

Yet others feel that such limitation also offer an opportunity for improving their management techniques.

Especially in making long-term loans, the borrower as well as the lender should be thinking of: (1) the net earning power of the borrowing company, (2) the capability of its management, (3) the long range prospects of the company, and (4) the long range prospects of the industry of which the company is a part. Such factors often mean that limitation increase as the duration of the loan increases.

What Kinds of Limitation?

The kinds of limitations, which an owner-manager finds set upon the company depends, to a great extent, on the company. If the company is a good risk, only minimum limitations need be set. A poor risk, of course, is different. Its limitation should be greater than those of a stronger company.

Look now for a few moments at the kinds of limitations and restrictions which the lender may set. Knowing what they are can help you see how they affect your operations.

The limitations which you will usually run into when you borrow money are:

(1) Repayment terms.

(2) Pledging or the use of security.

(3) Periodic reporting.

A loan agreement, as you may already know, is a tailor-made document covering, or referring to, all the terms and conditions of the loan. With it, the lender does two things: (1) protects position as a creditor (keeps that position in as protected a state as it was on the date the loan was made) and (2) assures repayment according to the terms.

The lender reasons that the borrower's business should generate enough funds to repay the loan while taking care of other needs. The lender considers that cash inflow should be great enough to do this without hurting the working capital of the borrower.

Covenants - Negative and Positive

The actual restrictions in a loan agreement come under a section known as covenants. Negative covenants are things which the borrower may not do without prior approval from the lender. Some examples are: further additions to the borrower's total debt, non pledge to others of the borrower's assets and issuance of dividends in excess of the terms of the loan agreement

On the other hand, positive covenants spell out things which the borrower must do. Some examples are: (1) maintenance of a minimum net working capital, (2) carrying of adequate insurance, (3) repaying the loan according to the terms of the agreement, and (4) supplying the lender with financial statements and reports.

Overall, however, loan agreements may be amended from time to time and exceptions made. Certain provisions may be waived from one year to the next with the consent of the lender.

You Can Negotiate

Next time you go to borrow money, thrash out the lending terms before you sign. It is good practice no matter how badly you may need the money. Ask to see the papers in advance of the loan closing. Legitimate lenders are glad to cooperate.

Chances are that the lender may "give" some on the terms. Keep in mind also that, while your are mulling over the terms, you may want to get the advice of your associates and outside advisors. In short, try to get terms which you know your company can live with. Remember, however that once the terms have been agreed upon and the loan is made you are bound by them.

The Loan Application

Now that you have read about the various aspects of the lending process and are ready to apply for a loan. Banks and other private lending institutions, require a loan application on which you list certain information about your business

Evaluating the Application

Once you have supplied the necessary information, the next step in the borrowing process is the evaluation of your application. The officer considers this kind of thing when determining whether to grant or refuse the loan:

The borrower's debt paying record to suppliers, banks, home mortgage holders, and other creditors.

The ratio of the borrower's debt to net worth.

The past earnings of the company.

The value and conditions of the collateral which the borrower offers for security.

7. Effective Business Management Strategies

Manage a business effectively, manage staff effectively, is the key to the establishment and growth of the business. The key to successful management is to examine the marketplace environment and create employment and profit opportunities that provide the potential growth and financial viability of the business. Despite the importance of management, this area is often misunderstood and poorly implemented, primarily because people focus on the output rather than the process of management.

Toward the end of the 1980s, business managers became absorbed in improving product quality, sometimes ignoring their role vis-a-vis personnel. The focus was on reducing costs and increasing output, while ignoring the long-term benefits of motivating personnel. This shortsighted view tended to increase profits in the short term, but created a dysfunctional long-term business environment.

Simultaneously with the increase in concern about quality, entrepreneurship attracted the attention of business. A sudden wave of successful entrepreneurs seemed to render earlier management concepts obsolete. The popular press focused on the new cult heroes Steve Jobs and Steve Wozniack (creators and developers of the Apple Computer) while ignoring the marketing and organizing talents of Mike Markula, the executive responsible for Apple's business plan. The story of two guys selling their Volkswagen bus to build the first Apple computer was more romantic than that of the organizational genius that enabled Apple to develop, market and ship its products while rapidly becoming a major corporation.

In large businesses, effective manage business skills requires planning. Planning is essential for developing a firm's potential. However, many small businesses do not recognize the need for long-range plans, because the small number of people involved in operating the business implies equal responsibility in the planning and decision-making processes. Nevertheless, the need for planning is as important in a small business as it is in a large one.

This guide focuses on the importance of good management practices. Specifically, it addresses the responsibilities of managing the external and internal environments.

MANAGING THE EXTERNAL ENVIRONMENT

Three decades ago, Alvin Toffler suggested that the vision of the citizen in the tight grip of an omnipotent bureaucracy would be replaced by an organizational structure of ad-hocracy. The traditional business organization implied a social contract between employees and employers. By adhering to a fixed set of obligations and sharply defined roles and responsibilities, employees received a predefined set of rewards.

The organizational structure that Toffler predicted in 1970 became the norm 20 years later, and with it came changed concepts of authority. As organizations became more transitory, the authority of the organization and firm was replaced by the authority of the individual manager. This entrepreneurial management model is now being replicated throughout society. As a result, the individual business owner must internalize ever increasing organizational functions.

Another change in today's business environment is dealing with government agencies. Their effect on the conduct of business most recently appears to have increased. As industries fail to achieve high levels of ethical behavior or individual businesses exhibit specific lapses, the government rushes in to fill the breach with its regulations.

MANAGING THE INTERNAL ENVIRONMENT

HUMAN RESOURCE ISSUES

Ensuring Open Communications

Effective communications play an integral role in managing and operating any successful business. With open communications changes and their effects on the organization are quickly shared. Your firm then has the time and skills needed to respond to changes and take advantage of evolving opportunities.

The following checklist addressing how you would respond to an employee's suggestion provides an assessment of the communication process in your business. Place a check next to the statements that are commonly heard in your business.

Statement

Face facts it's unrealistic. -----

Who else has done it? -----

It's not your problem. -----

Fill out form XX/xx revised. -----

It won't work. -----

Bring it to the committee. -----

We don't have the time. -----

We tried it before and it failed. -----

You think what? You're joking! -----

Everybody knows that that's foolish. -----

We can't afford to think about it. -----

Don't you have better things to do? -----

Are you some kind of a radical? -----

We're too small/big for that. -----

Impossible; our main product line would be obsolete. -----

The boss would never consider it. -----

It's contrary to company policy. -----

Carefully consider any statements that you have checked. This may indicate that management is inflexible and unresponsive to employee suggestions. Management that is unable to respond immediately to changes in the market signals an inflexible unstable firm. In the rapidly changing business environment such management can mean eventual failure for your business. If you haven't developed such a checklist do so. It will help you determine if and where adjustments are needed in your management staff.

Balancing Schedules Stress and Personnel

Without organization and good management the compressed time schedules associated with modern business can cause stress and make extraordinary demands on people. An effective management structure can reduce stress and channel the productive capacity of employees into business growth and profits.

Setting Duties Tasks and Responsibilities

An organization is characterized by the nature and determination of employees' duties tasks and responsibilities. While many organizations use different methods for determining these it is essential that they be clearly defined.

The core of any organization is its people and their functions. Duties tasks and responsibilities often evolve in an ad hoc manner. A typical firm starts with a few people often one performing all duties. As the firm grows others are hired to fill specific roles often on a functional basis. Roles that were handled by consultants and specialists outside the firm now are handled internally. As new needs emerge new roles are developed.

Just as an emerging business develops an accounting system it should also develop a human resource system. For instance the following employee information should be available and checked for accuracy at least once each year.

- Name

- Address

- Nationality (immigration status)

- Marital status and dependents

- Hire date

- Company job history:

- Title and code

- Performance

- Location

- Salary rate and history

- Education including degrees

- Specialty training

- Transcripts as appropriate

- Pre-employment work experience:

- Key responsibilities and levels

- Professional licenses or certificates

- Professional publication and speaking engagements

- Teaching experience

- Language abilities:

- Reading

- Writing

- Speaking

- Leadership evidence:

- Company

- Civic

- Other

- Relocation preferences and limitations

- Travel experience and preferences

- Career goals

Review your personnel files periodically to ensure that the information is correct and current. Implement a system that will make updating personnel files a fairly simple routine yet confidential process.

Business Team

The apex of an effective organization lies in developing the business team. Such a team involves delegating authority and increasing productivity. Assess the effectiveness of your business team with the following checklist:

The leader of the team is respected by the members. -----

The abilities of all team members are respected. -----

A team spirit is evident through activities. -----

Individual members compensate for weaknesses in each other. -----

Jokes are not disparaging. -----

A genuine feeling of being part of the best is exuded. -----

The work area is self-delineated and reflects a spirit. -----

Mistakes result in corrective action not retribution. -----

Each member understands the importance of his or her contribution. -----

The team can explore new areas of activity. -----

Security of employment is evident. -----

Controlling Conflict

Another key to successful management lies in controlling conflict. Conflict cannot be eliminated from either the business or the interpersonal activities of the enterprise. A measure of the organization's success is the degree to which conflict can be exposed and the energies associated with it channeled to develop the firm. Although establishing policies and procedures represents the tangible aspect of organization and management the mechanisms to tolerate and embody challenges to the established operation serve as the real essence of a firm that will survive and prosper.

Structural Issues

Organization

The effectiveness of a particular organizational form depends on a variety of internal and external events for example:

Competitors (number or activity)

Technology (internal or external)

Regulatory environment

Customer characteristics

Supplier characteristics

Economic environment

Key employees

Growth

Strategy (including new products and markets)

Even though you may discover that certain events are affecting your business be careful not to change the organizational structure of your firm without discussing it with your management team. Employees generally can accomplish goals despite organizational structures imposed by management. Because restructuring involves spending a lot of time learning new rules implementing a new organizational structure is costly.

Structure

The essence of a successful organization can be more simply summarized than implemented. The following checklist can help you determine measures to ensure your management structure is adequate. Check the entries that apply to your firm and also find out what measures your company needs to take to improve its management structure.

Key market and customers are understood. -----

Technology is mastered. -----

Key objectives are articulated and shared. -----

Major functions are identified and staffed. -----

A hierarchy of relationships is established. -----

A business team is in place and functioning. -----

Measurable results are well above industry standards. -----

Employees are the best source of new hires. -----

Policy and Procedural Issues

Authority

The central element of organizational management is authority. Through authority your firm develops the structure necessary to achieve its objectives.

A. L. Stinchcombe summarized the role of authority succinctly when he stated any administrative system that decides on the use of resources is also a system of authority directing the activities of people.

The authority that once was conferred by either owning a small business or having a position in the bureaucracy of a larger firm has been replaced by technical competence (including that of forming and running the business). Forces external to your business may emphasize the elements of granted versus earned authority. Once the owner-manager controlled the entire business but suppliers customers unions and the government have severely limited the ability of the business owner-manager to take independent action.

A primary component of authority is the exercise of control within the organization. A thorough system of controls ensures the firm's operation and provides a mechanism for imposing authority. Internal controls include the provision that authority be delegated and circumscribed; examples of these provisions follow. Place a check by the provisions that apply to your firm. Consider implementing controls over areas that you have not checked.

Approval for disbursements of cash and regular accounting. -----

Reconciliation of bank statements. -----

Periodic count and reconciliation of inventory records. -----

Approval of pricing policies and exemptions. -----

Approval of credit policies and exemptions. -----

Review of expense and commission accounts. -----

Approval of purchasing and receiving policies. -----

Review of payments to vendors and employees. -----

Approval of signature authorities for payments. -----

Review of policies. -----

Delegation is a key to the effective exercise of authority in your business. By delegating limited authority to accomplish specific tasks the talents of employees in the organization can be used to upgrade the skills and experience of the manager. The following checklist enables you to determine if you are taking advantage of opportunities to delegate authority.

Is your time consumed by daily chores? -----

Do you have time for the following:

- Training and development of subordinates? -----

- Planning? -----

- Coordinating and controlling work of subordinates? -----

- Visiting customers and subordinates regularly? -----

- Remaining involved in new product development? -----

- Visiting branch locations regularly? -----

- Attending business meetings outside your business? -----

- Participating in civic affairs? -----

Is no one on your staff as good as you are? -----

To effectively delegate responsibility and authority in your organization you must:

Accept the power of delegation.

Know the capabilities of subordinates.

Ensure that specific training is available.

Select specific responsibilities to be delegated.

Clearly define the extent and limits of delegation.

Match each with necessary authority.

Provide periodic monitoring and interest.

Restrain the impulse to insist on how to do something.

Remember there are many ways to accomplish a specific objective.

Assess results and provide appropriate feedback.

Praise and criticize.

The skills and abilities of each level of authority can be increased by effectively delegating authority throughout any organization.

Operating Reports

Operating reports form the organizational basis of your business. Such reports mirror the organization its structure and function. They define key relationships between employees and can either minimize or increase organizational stress.

For many businesses the following reports form the basis for analyzing the specific areas of a business (the frequency of each report depends on the nature size and organization of your business). Check the reports your firm currently generates.

Consider creating reporting systems where they are lacking.

Case reports (daily, weekly, monthly) -----

New orders and backlog (weekly, monthly) -----

Shipments/sales (weekly, monthly) -----

Employment (monthly) -----

Inventory out of stock (weekly, monthly) -----

Product quality (weekly, monthly) -----

Accounts receivable aging accounts (monthly) -----

Weekly overdue accounts -----

Returns and allowances (monthly) -----

Production (weekly, monthly) -----

Reporting must be kept current to allow for timely identification and correction of problems before serious damage to the organization occurs.

Too much reporting as well as inappropriate reporting can be as destructive as too little reporting. For instance the CEO of a major industrial firm who receives daily production and inventory reports by model can lose his or her ability to maintain an overall perspective. Thus operating managers must attempt to identify and solve local problems and take advantage of local opportunities within their own authority. Inappropriate reporting compromises management's ability to leverage individual skills and abilities.

Operating reports not only provide essential data that enable management to accomplish its objectives they also focus staff's attention on the organization's goals. If reporting is not taken seriously employees may deal with customers suppliers and each other in a similarly trivial manner.

To avoid inappropriate reporting review reporting policies annually to ensure that reports are appropriate and contain the information needed to make sound management decisions.

Conclusion

Successful management is founded on the mastery of a myriad of details. While management schools teach the importance of focusing attention on major issues affecting the business practical managers realize the major issues are the variety of small aspects that form the business. In an increasingly structured society inattention to even one minor detail can result in significant disruption of the business or even its failure.

Checklist For An Effective Organization

The following checklist will help you identify and determine the effectiveness of the management and organizational structure of the firm. If you answer yes to most of the following questions you are effectively managing your firm. A no answer indicates that you need to focus on this management issue.

yes/no

Are responsibilities clear and matched by authority?

Is your business structure clear yet flexible? -----

Are communications focused on finding solutions rather than placing blame? -----

Do people have the information and resources necessary to do an excellent job? -----

Do you and your employees care about the business? -----

Does staff come in early and stay late on their own initiative? -----

Are mechanisms for conflict resolution working? -----

Is disorder minimized and channeled? -----

Can people joke with and about each other and you? -----

Does a corporate plan spell out the firm's vision? -----

Do employees pitch in unasked during a crisis? -----

Do customers and suppliers prefer to do business with you? -----

8. How to Cut Costs In Your Business

Increasing profits through reduce costs and cost cutting must be based on the concept of an organized, planned program. Unless adequate records are maintained through a proper accounting system, there can be no basis for ascertaining and analyzing costs.

Cost cutting is not simply attempting to slash any and all expenses unmethodically. The owner-manager must understand the nature of expenses and how expenses inter-relate with sales, inventories, cost of goods sold, gross profits, and net profits.

Reduce costs does not mean only the reduction of specific expenses. You can achieve greater profits through more efficient use of the expense dollar. Some of the ways you do this are by increasing the average sale per customer, by effectively using display space and thereby increasing sales volume per square foot, by getting a larger return for your advertising and sales promotion dollar, and by improving your internal methods and procedures.

Profit is in danger when good merchandising and

cost control do not go hand in hand. A big sales volume does not necessarily mean a big profit, as one retailer, Carl Jones, learned.

Jones's pride was stocking stylish and well assorted lines of merchandise. Each year, sales volume increased. This increase was attributed to good merchandise which Jones felt took care of the steady rise in expenses.

But Mr. Jones began to have doubts when he found it necessary to get bank loans more often than had been his practice. When he discussed the problem with his banker, Jones was advised to check expenses. As the banker said, "A large and increasing sales volume often creates the appearance of prosperity while behind-the-scene expenses are eating up the profit."

Paying The Right Price

Your goal should be to pay the right price for prosperity. Determining that price for your operation goes beyond knowing what your expenses are. Reducing expenses to increase profit requires you to obtain the most efficient use of the expense dollar.

Look, for example, at the payroll expense. Salesclerks are paid to sell goods, and their productivity is the key to reducing the payroll cost.

If you train a salesclerk to make multiple sales at higher unit prices, you increase productivity and your profits without adding dollars to your payroll expenses. Or, if four salesclerks can be trained to sell the amount previously sold by seven, the payroll can be cut by three persons.

An understanding of the worth of each expense item comes from experience and an analysis of records. Adequate records tell what has happened. Their analysis provide facts which can help you set realistic goals, you are paying the right price for your store's prosperity.

Analyze Your Expenses

Sometimes you cannot cut an increase item. But you can get more from it and thus increase your profits. In analyzing your expenses, you should use percentages rather than actual dollar amounts.

For example, if you increase sales and keep the dollar amount of an expense the same, you have decreased that expense as a percentage of sales.

When you decrease your cost percentage, you increase your percentage of profit.

On the other hand, if your sales volume remains the same, you can increase the percentage of profit by reducing a specific item of expense. Your goal, of course, is to do both: to decrease specific expenses and increase their productive worth at the same time.

Before you can determine whether cutting expenses will increase profits, you need information about your operation. This information can be obtained only if you have an adequate recordkeeping system. Such records will provide the figures to prepare a profit and loss statement (preferably monthly for most retail businesses), a budget, break-even calculations, and evaluations of your operating ratios compared with those of similar types of business.

Break-even

A useful method for making expense comparisons is break-even analysis. Break-even is the point at which gross profit equals expenses. In a business year, it is the time at which your sales volume has become sufficient to enable your over-all operation to start showing a profit.

Once your sales volume reached the break-even point, your fixed expenses are covered. Beyond the break-even point, every dollar of sales should earn you an equivalent additional profit percentage.

It is important to remember that once sales pass the break-even point, the fixed expenses percentage goes down as the sales volume goes up. Also the operating profit percentage increases at the same rate as the percentage rate for fixed expenses decreases - provided, of course, that variable expenses are kept in line.

Locating Reducible Expenses

Your profit and loss (or income) statement provides a summary of expense information and is the focal point in locating expenses that can be cut. Therefore, the information should be as current as possible. As a report of what has already been spent, a P and L statement alerts you to expense items that bear watching in the present business period. If you get a P and L statement only at the end of the year, you should consider having one prepared more often. At the end of each quarter might be often enough for some firms. Ideally, you can get the most recent information from a monthly P and L.

Regardless of the frequency, for the most information two P and L statements should be prepared. One statement should report the sales, expenses, profits and/or loss of your operations cumulatively for the current business year to date. The other should report on the same items for the last complete month or quarter. Each of the statements should also carry the following information:

(1) this year's figures and each item as a percentage of sales.

(2) last year's figures and the percentages.

(3) the difference between last year and this year - over or under.

(4) budgeted figures and the respective percentages.

(5) the difference between this year and the budgeted figures - over and under.

(6) average percentages for your line of business (industry operating ratio) when available, and

(7) the difference between your annual percentages

and the industry ratios - under or over.

This information allows you to locate expense variation in three ways: (1) by comparing this year to last year, (2) by comparing expenses to your own budgeted figures, and (3) by comparing your percentages to the operating ratios for your line of business. The important basis for comparison is the percentage figure. It represents a common denominator for all three methods. When you have indicated the percentage variations, you should then study the dollar amounts to determine what line of operative action is needed.

Because your cost cutting will come largely form variable expenses, you should make sure that they are flagged on your P and L statements. Variable expenses are those which fluctuate with the increase or decrease of sales volume. Some of them are: advertising, delivery, wrapping supplies, sales salaries, commissions, and payroll taxes. Fixed expenses are those which stay the same regardless of sales volume. Among them are: your salary, salaries for permanent non-selling employees (for example, the bookkeeper), depreciation, rent, and utilities.

Taking cost cutting Action

When you have located a problem expense area, the next step obviously is to reduce that cost so as to increase your profit. A key to the effectiveness of your cost-cutting action is the worth of the various expenditures. As long as you know the worth of your expenditures, you can profit by making small improvements in expenses. Keep an open eye and an open mind. It is better to do a spot analysis once a month than to wait several months and then do a detailed study. Take action as soon as possible. You can refine your cost-cutting action as you go along.

9. Special Free Bonuses (download links are provided)

a. Excel Financial Projections Creator - simply type in your business' details and assumptions and it will automatically produce a comprehensive set of financial projections for your specific business, including: Start-Up Expenses, Projected Balance Sheet, Projected Cash Flow Statement, Financial Ratios Analysis, Projected Profit and Loss Statement, Break Even Analysis, and many more.

Copy the following link to your browser and save the file to your PC:

http://www.bizmove.com/bp/projections.xlsx

Detailed guide that will walk you step by step and show you exactly how to effectively use the above Excel Financial Projections Creator.

Copy the following link to your browser and save the file to your PC:

http://www.bizmove.com/bp/projections-guide.doc

b. MS Word format version of the business plan template - Extensive business plan template in MS word format - this is a high quality, full blown business plan template complete with detailed instructions and all related spread sheets. Allows you to prepare a professional business plan.

Copy the following link to your browser and save the file to your PC:

http://www.bizmove.com/tools/Startup-Business-Plan-Template.docx

c. Simple business plan template in MS Word format - allows you to craft a good business plan quickly and easily.

Copy the following link to your browser and save the file to your PC:

http://www.bizmove.com/tools/bptemplate.docx

d. Small Business Management: Essential Ingredients for Success (eBook) - Learn effective business management tricks, secrets and shortcuts to make your business a success.

Copy the following link to your browser and save the file to your PC:

http://www.bizmove.com/bp/management.pdf

e. Business Plan Training Course (Online Video)

This training course discusses the creation of a business plan. It explains the importance of business planning defines and describes the business plan outline and its components thus enabling you to develop a very good business plan.

Copy the following link to your browser and save the file to your PC:

http://www.bizmove.com/video//business-plan-training-course.htm

f. How To Find And Attract Investors Training Course (Online Video):

This self-paced training video will show you how to find and attract investors. Topics include determining the need for outside financing, defining what an investor is and where to find them, explaining the investment process and understanding investor expectations.

Copy the following link to your browser and save the file to your PC:

http://www.bizmove.com/business-training/how-to-find-and-attract-investors.htm

g. How to Start a Small Business Manual (PDF eBook) - a practical guide that will walk you step by step through all the essential phases of starting your own business. The book is packed with guides, worksheets and checklists. These strategies are absolutely crucial to your business' success yet are simple and easy to apply.

Copy the following link to your browser and save the file to your PC:

https://www.bizmove.com/toolkit/start-business.htm

h. How to Be a Great Manager and Leader (Video Guide) - Learn how to improve your leadership skills and become a better manager and leader. Be the boss people want to give 200 percent for. In this video you'll discover 120 powerful tips and strategies to motivate and inspire your people to bring out the best in them.

Watch it here:

https://www.bizmove.com/toolkit/leader.htm

i. How to Better Manage Yourself for Success (Video Guide) - You are responsible for everything that happens in your life. Learn to accept total responsibility for yourself. If you don't manage yourself, then you are letting others have control of your life. In this video you'll discover 90 powerful tips and strategies to better manage yourself for success.

Watch it here:

https://www.bizmove.com/toolkit/self-management.htm

# # # #

www.ingramcontent.com/pod-product-compliance
Lightning Source LLC
Chambersburg PA
CBHW071207220526
45468CB00002B/524